# WAVERLEY – *Last of the Clyde*

Andrew Clark

*Waverley* off Cumbrae in August 2000.

First published in the United Kingdom, 2015,
by Stenlake Publishing Ltd.
Telephone: 01290 551122
www.stenlake.co.uk

ISBN 9781840337112

TV personality Bill Tennent launches the first *Waverley* appeal in 1974, flanked by George Train, Douglas McGowan, Terry Sylvester and Peter Reid.

## Acknowledgements

Photographs were kindly provided by A.E. Bennett, Douglas Brown, Stuart Cameron, James Christie, Douglas McGowan, David Neill, John Newth, Andy O'Brian, John Openshaw, Stephen Roberts, Eric Schofield, David Scott, the J.T.A. Brown Collection and the *Eastern Daily Press*. Images from the Sinclair Collection are reproduced by courtesy of the Scottish Maritime Museum, Irvine. Additional help came from Leslie Brown, Derek Crawford, Alex Forrest, Graeme Hogg, Fraser MacHaffie, Iain MacLeod, Ian Ramsay and Lawrie Sinclair.

# Introduction

If anyone had predicted, 40 years ago, that *Waverley* would be sailing today, they would probably have been ridiculed. The enthusiasts who took ownership of the ailing 27-year old paddler in the mid 1970s barely had their sights on the next day, never mind the next week or next year. They had no experience of ship ownership and next to no money. Their decision to accept an offer from the state-controlled ferry operator Caledonian MacBrayne was founded on hope, not reason. But they learned quickly, they worked tirelessly and they overcame setbacks, always with the goal of keeping *Waverley* sailing rather than consigning her to static preservation. Thanks to their efforts the sound of paddles, the smell of steam and the sight of her engines remain as distinctive as they were on 22nd May 1975, that auspicious day when she set sail from Glasgow on a 'doon the watter' trip to Ardrishaig – her first voyage under the aegis of the Paddle Steamer Preservation Society (PSPS).

In the late 1960s there had been better candidates for preservation. Of all the surviving excursion steamers, *Waverley* – the youngest – had the least personality. But no one was prepared for the speed with which Britain's fleet of paddle steamers was being wound down – and no one would receive a better offer than the sale, for a symbolic £1, of the last sea-going representative of them all. With her twin funnels and traditional fan-shaped paddle-box, *Waverley* was somehow iconic. During a hull survey late in 1974 she was found to be more solidly built than had been thought possible for a ship dating from the immediate post-war era, when materials were in short supply. For the quarter-century after 1975 she was nurtured, cleaned, cajoled, modified and, at the end of the 1990s, virtually reconstructed, courtesy of a £5.5m Heritage Lottery Fund grant.

If nothing lasts for ever, there must surely come a time when *Waverley* joins the ranks of her distinguished predecessors whose bridge telegraphs finally rang 'finished with engines'. So let's live for today and celebrate not just the opportunities she offers to enjoy a sail round our coastline, but also the achievements of successive generations of crew, shore staff and volunteers who, by their dedication and skill, have kept *Waverley* going.

Looking back on the events of 1973-75, you have to wonder what on earth CalMac thought they were doing by handing *Waverley* to a bunch of amateurs. Did they expect her to remain tied up, a monument to the past? The inside story will never be known, but thanks to Douglas McGowan and Terry Sylvester, two commercially minded enthusiasts, public opinion was stirred to the point where CalMac simply could not sell *Waverley* for scrap. McGowan and Sylvester realised the paddler could be marketed as a modern-day tourist attraction, not a museum. It was they who brought together the 'holy trinity' – the PSPS as major shareholder, the not-for-profit Waverley Steam Navigation Company as legal owner and, from 1980, Waverley Excursions Ltd as operator. This division of responsibilities holds good today, but the moral owners of the ship remain the ordinary members of the PSPS, a much older group of individuals in 2015 than they were in 1975.

*Waverley* would not have survived her first two decades of preservation without the industry and ship handling skills of Captain David Neill, but those skills were sometimes compromised by a flair for risk-taking, of which the Gantocks disaster (when the ship was almost fatally grounded off Dunoon in 1977) was the most unfortunate example. There were other mistakes, all of them now airbrushed out of the *Waverley* story by the passing of time. By 2000 the 'demigods' of the preservation era had stood down from day-to-day management. While they continue to provide a rallying point for a *Waverley* 'old guard' – people who hanker for a time when the sun always shone – the ship is now in the hands of people who understand that the nature of the business has changed.

Fifteen years ago the value of onboard ticket sales was still a significant percentage of the total. Today there are far more advance bookings, principally through the internet, a phenomenon unknown to the ship's previous managers. *Waverley* has to compete in a leisure market more crowded – and much more sophisticated – than it was a generation ago. The regulatory environment has become more restrictive, throwing up all sorts of hurdles for a relic of the steam age. Fuel prices have risen much faster than ticket prices. Non-earning positioning runs that *Waverley* once took in her stride now look hopelessly impractical. It has reached the stage where, unless she earns £12,000 each day she goes out (enough to cover running costs, with some extra for winter overhaul), she loses money.

All this helps to explain why the ship's management, recently led by WEL chairman David Kells and chief executive Kathleen O'Neill, began to adopt an increasingly hard-nosed approach. The purpose of the operation is no longer to stretch the season as a means of generating income – the 'keep sailing at all costs' policy of the 1980s and 1990s. No, by reducing the number of sailing days, the ship may actually have a better chance of survival. The guiding principle has become: every sailing day must have the potential to be profitable. If you risk losing money, it may be better to keep the ship tied up.

It is one of the truisms of *Waverley*'s existence that every season is 'make-or-break'. The public at large do not owe her a living, and may not bail her out again to the extent they did in 1974 and 1976. Since the disastrous 2012 season, when the future really did look bleak, the balance of income and expenditure has shown signs of improvement. *Waverley*'s story of survival continues, and everyone who steps onto her decks plays a part in it.

Andrew Clark
Glasgow, July 2015

Stranded on the Gantocks in July 1977.

Mention *Waverley* to anyone with an interest in ships, and "the world's last sea-going paddle steamer" will almost certainly come to mind – a two-funnelled vessel built on the Clyde in 1947 and operated since 1974 by a company representing the Paddle Steamer Preservation Society. To previous generations *Waverley* conjured different associations, all similarly inspired by the hero of Sir Walter Scott's first novel. The first ship to receive the name was built at Dumbarton in 1828 during the earliest days of steam navigation. A spartan little paddler, she plied on the Glasgow, Greenock and Helensburgh route until she was sold to the Humber in 1837. The next *Waverley*, built in 1885 for the Campbells of Kilmun, lasted only two years on the Clyde before transferring to the Bristol Channel. The third bearer of the name, pictured above in 1937, was one of the fastest and most popular steamers of the early 20th century. Dating from 1899, she served as the North British Railway Company's flagship in the pre-1914 era, the 'golden years' of rivalry between railway-owned fleets on the Firth. Employed on excursions from Craigendoran, the NBR railhead on the north bank of the Clyde, she became particularly associated with the service to Arrochar at the head of Long Long, passing in 1923 into the ownership of the London and North Eastern Railway. The photographs on the next two pages, showing crew (with Captain John Gray) and passengers on her foredeck, date from the early and late 1920s.

WAVERLEY
GLASGOW

The 1899 *Waverley* undertook minesweeping duties in both world wars. Pictured during the 1914-18 conflict in convoy with the P. & A. Campbell paddler *Lady Moyra*, she was sunk in May 1940 by German bombers while attempting to evacuate British soldiers from Dunkirk. Around 300 servicemen were drowned. The loss was commemorated in May 1980 when her 1947 successor visited the English Channel for a ceremony overseen by Captain John Cameron (right), who served as master of both ships. The *Waverley* we know today has often been touted as a "replacement" for the paddler lost at Dunkirk, and a brass plaque to that effect was mounted on her aft deckhouse. But the 1899 *Waverley* had been laid up throughout the summer of 1939 as an economy measure. The LNER's war losses included not just the 1899 paddler but also her fleet mate *Marmion*, sunk off Harwich in April 1941. In effect the 1947 *Waverley* replaced two steamers – though Admiralty compensation for their loss accounted for only a quarter of her £105,850 contract price.

The reasoning behind *Waverley*'s old-fashioned design has long been the subject of speculation. Pictured after her launch at A. & J. Inglis' Pointhouse Yard on the upper Clyde on 2nd October 1946, the new paddler – the last to be built for Clyde service – had many time-served features, including three-crank diagonal engines and American elm paddle floats (eight on each side). Despite up-to-date features such as a raked stem and cruiser stern, she was in many respects a smaller version of her 1931 LNER fleet mate *Jeanie Deans*. The order for the new steamer came in the immediate aftermath of the Second World War, when most ship owners were turning to cheaper, easier-to-maintain diesel technology and a more utilitarian look. *Waverley*'s distinctive profile, with covered wheelhouse, brown upper works, and deckhouses mounted with heavenward-pointing davits, owed much to existing Inglis designs for a pre-war paddler, which were quickly adapted in 1945-46 for the new ship and for the re-modelling of the Craigendoran paddlers that survived the war.

After fitting out at her builder's yard near the mouth of the River Kelvin, three miles from the centre of Glasgow, *Waverley* was towed in February 1947 to Greenock's Victoria Harbour, where the engineering company Rankin & Blackmore fitted her with a Scotch boiler and a magnificent steam engine. The absence of the aft funnel in this picture suggests installation of the machinery is still under way. Designed as a coal-burner, *Waverley* was converted in 1957 to burn heavy fuel oil. Her double-ended boiler – now preserved at the Scottish Maritime Museum in Irvine – was replaced in 1981 by a Babcock shore boiler, which could be 'flashed up' from cold in four hours (as opposed to the 24 hours taken by its predecessor). It reduced fuel consumption by a fifth. In 2000 the Babcock was replaced by twin Cochran boilers heated by smoke-tubes: if one boiler breaks down, the other can still provide steam for a reduced speed. *Waverley*'s chief engineer for her first 22 years was William Summers. In 1975 he came out of retirement to help launch the preservation era.

This photograph of *Waverley*'s forward deckhouse was taken during a trial run in June 1947, shortly before her first public sailing. It shows the wood-effect paintwork, known as 'scumbling', that – along with funnel colours of red, white and black – distinguished the LNER paddlers from the yellow-and-black funnelled steamers of the Caledonian Steam Packet Company. *Waverley* lasted only one season in her original colours. After nationalisation of Britain's railways on 1st January 1948, a gradual process of standardisation was applied, and the handsome colours that had graced the Craigendoran fleet since the early 1880s disappeared. Funnels were painted yellow and black in 1948. In 1953 *Waverley* became the first former LNER paddler to have her deckhouses painted white; her paddle-boxes followed suit in 1958. All this was later reversed. In 1972, following pressure from steamer enthusiasts, her paddle-boxes reverted to black, and in 1975, her first year in preserved hands, she re-appeared with her original tricolour funnel colouring. 'Scumbled' deckhouses returned as a final touch of authenticity in 2000, when *Waverley* underwent the first phase of a rebuild supported by the Heritage Lottery Fund.

On her maiden voyage on Monday 16th June 1947 *Waverley* sailed on the route for which she was primarily intended – from Craigendoran and Dunoon to Lochgoilhead (where she is pictured leaving the pier astern) and Arrochar. The sailing, with connections from Largs, Millport and Rothesay, was part of the long-established Three Lochs Tour, a circular journey taking in two scenic sea lochs, Loch Goil and Loch Long, and the freshwater Loch Lomond. From Arrochar excursionists would cross, on foot or by coach, the narrow strip of land to Tarbet, from where a smaller paddle steamer took them along the 'bonnie banks' to Balloch at the south end of Loch Lomond, with train connection back to Craigendoran or Glasgow. With rare exceptions *Waverley* sailed to Arrochar six times a week in 1947. This frequency subsequently dwindled. After being declared unsafe, Lochgoilhead Pier closed in July 1965, and by 1972 the service had dropped to once a week. With the closure of Arrochar Pier at the end of that summer, the Three Lochs Tour lapsed. Nevertheless, for holidaymakers at coast resorts in the post-war era, it was one of the most popular and spectacular excursions on the Clyde.

A Blue Star liner passes Bowling on her way down the River Clyde to the open sea – a common sight in the days when Glasgow was a busy port. In the foreground is Bowling Harbour, a haven for Clyde steamers during their winter layup. What the camera has captured is the moment in the spring of 1948 when funnel colours were standardised after railway nationalisation on January 1st. *Waverley* has already exchanged the distinctive red, white and black funnel colouring of the LNER for the yellow with black top of the British Transport Commission, the state-controlled organisation that had legal ownership of the Craigendoran fleet until their transfer to the Caledonian Steam Packet Company in 1951. *Jeanie Deans*, lying ahead of *Waverley*, will shortly undergo the same transformation. Thereafter the only obvious trace of their LNER origins was the steel hoop around the funnels that once marked the border between white and red.

The former LNER fleet soaks up the evening sun at Craigendoran in June 1948: (left to right) *Talisman, Lucy Ashton, Jeanie Deans, Waverley*. Despite the change in ownership brought about by nationalisation at the beginning of the year, all four steamers went about their work in much the same way as they had the previous summer. Having celebrated her diamond jubilee on May 29th with a Clyde River Steamer Club charter, the veteran *Lucy Ashton* continued as Gourock ferry and second Dunoon vessel. This was to be her last year in service. *Talisman*, built in 1935, provided the twice-a-day service to Dunoon and Rothesay, with an extra sailing on Saturdays. She had had a good war, but her pioneering diesel-electric machinery threw up periodic problems, and after re-engining in 1953-54 she was assigned to the Wemyss Bay-Millport run, in which capacity she served reliably until her demise at the end of the 1966 season. *Jeanie Deans'* main destination in the summer of 1948 was the Kyles of Bute, stopping at Tighnabruaich and Auchenlochan. *Waverley* continued to function as the north bank's 'cruise boat', which meant Lochgoilhead and Arrochar six days a week, plus morning and evening runs to Rothesay. It took several years for north bank crews and service schedules to be properly integrated with steamers based at Gourock on the south bank of the Clyde.

Once curiosity about the fleet's latest addition had subsided, *Waverley* was eclipsed in the popularity stakes by older, more familiar steamers which, unlike her, had served their country with distinction in the war and represented a cherished link with the past. *Waverley*, it was said, had been cheaply built, and was not always well maintained. She was, nevertheless, the fastest paddler on the Clyde. Having achieved 18.37 knots on trial, she could easily "dust" her rivals, as she appears intent on doing in this picture from the summer of 1948. Today she rarely exceeds 15 knots.

There is a palpable air of excitement on *Waverley*'s starboard sponson as she pulls away from Dunoon, with *Jeanie Deans* in hot pursuit and the former Williamson-Buchanan turbine steamer *Queen Mary II* (left) heading in the opposite direction on her way back to Glasgow. Such were the quirks of the post-nationalisation timetable that, on Saturday afternoons in the summer of 1949, it was not unusual for the two north bank paddlers to be heading simultaneously for Rothesay: *Waverley* (from Craigendoran) and *Jeanie* (from Gourock) sailed in competition with each other, with both scheduled to depart Dunoon around 5.30pm. What this photograph also reveals is that *Waverley* was built with open sponsons – an attractive feature, allowing passengers to go to the very edge of the paddle-box. By 1952 the sponsons had been railed off, a restriction that persists to this day. *Jeanie*'s were similarly off-limits in the post-war era, but *Talisman* and the 1934 *Caledonia* kept their open sponsons until their demise in the late 1960s. The downside of open sponsons was that the available deck space could affect the ship's stability if a crowd gathered on one side during the approach to a pier.

*Waverley* leaves Innellan at 5.55pm on Saturday 3rd September 1949, her last run of the day from Craigendoran to Rothesay. Having completed her Three Lochs Tour duties at 4.15, she would have left the north bank railhead at 4.50 and proceeded via Kilcreggan, Hunter's Quay, Kirn and Dunoon to Innellan and Rothesay. After a quick turnaround, doing her bit to clear the crowds of homeward-bound day-trippers, she would begin her return journey up-firth at 6.20, reaching Craigendoran by 8pm: all being well, the connecting train would pull in to Glasgow Queen Street an hour later. Craigendoran-based steamers were the most frequent callers at Innellan, a small community four miles south of Dunoon on the Cowal shoreline. Built in 1850 and extended in 1900, the pier was privately owned. At the time this photograph was taken, it was threatened with closure, the owner having recently died. Argyll County Council were prevailed upon to take it over, and Innellan continued to receive steamer calls until September 1972. The pier re-opened between March and October 1974 to convey workers to McAlpine's oil rig construction yard at Ardyne, but was subsequently dismantled – one of many Clyde piers that suffered from the march of progress.

During the 1950s *Waverley*'s cruise programme expanded – at the expense of her Arrochar trips, which were gradually reduced to twice a week. In 1953 she began a Monday sailing from Craigendoran through the Kyles of Bute to Brodick, Lamlash and Whiting Bay, the longest pier in the Clyde, where she is pictured on 19th July 1954. Lamlash Pier closed at the end of 1954 and Whiting Bay in 1961, but *Waverley* continued her 'Arran via the Kyles' cruise until 1971, latterly calling only at Brodick and then sailing towards Pladda at the south end of Arran. In 1955 she revived a popular pre-war cruise 'Round the Lochs and Firth of Clyde' – basically a sailing round Bute via Largs and Keppel in the first half of the day, and then, after calling at Rothesay at 2pm, a cruise to Loch Goil. It was around this time that *Waverley* reached her peak: under Captain Colin Mackay she achieved a reputation for punctuality and general smartness.

For her first 15 years *Waverley* (left of centre) received her annual overhaul at her birthplace, A. & J. Inglis' shipyard on the River Kelvin, which closed in 1963. For the winter of 1962-63 she was transferred to Harland & Wolff at Govan, and thereafter to Lamont of Port Glasgow. Since 1974 *Waverley* has been most commonly overhauled at Garvel Dry Dock, Greenock. In this view of Inglis' yard from *circa* 1955, she sits between a 'Maid' (on the slipway, left) and *Jeanie Deans* (foreground, right). The overhaul involved general repairs, paintwork, varnishing and engine maintenance. After the introduction of the four diesel-powered *Maids* in 1953, *Waverley*'s winter duties were few, the role of 'spare' vessel being assigned to *Talisman* or *Caledonia*. After retiring to harbour at the end of September, she would emerge from winter slumber in time for Easter weekend sailings – one exception being the spring of 1957, when her re-appearance was delayed by work on her conversion to burn oil fuel.

In her early years *Waverley* was certified to carry up to 1,350 passengers – a far cry from today's maximum of 860 as far as Rothesay, 800 to Tighnabruaich and 740 beyond. Her size made her useful for peak-holiday ferry duties usually undertaken by the smaller, more utilitarian *Maids* and car ferries. At the tail end of the season *Waverley* also found employment as a substitute for Gourock-based turbines on long-distance excursions (inset). The main picture shows her at Wemyss Bay in 1963 with a new aft funnel. Corrosion had necessitated the replacement of the forward funnel in 1961, and the aft funnel received similar treatment the following year. The new funnels, minus LNER 'hoops', were welded rather than riveted. Their extra weight caused a sag in the deck that resulted in the funnels being visibly out of alignment – a flaw that was not rectified until many years later. The riveted funnels she bears today date from 1999-2000, when she underwent the first phase of reconstruction at Great Yarmouth.

On Saturday 17th August 1963 *Waverley* remained tied up at Craigendoran, victim of an unofficial strike by her deck crew. The turbine steamer *Duchess of Montrose* was summoned to take over the paddler's roster, bringing her to the North Bank railhead for only the second time in her career (the first was in 1933). That morning *Waverley*'s seamen, supported by her firemen, had refused to work after the relief master dismissed one of their number for turning up late. During lengthy negotiations it transpired that the previous day, unbeknown to anyone else, the seaman had been granted a few hours' extra leave by the ship's captain, Hector Connell. All was resolved and the following morning *Waverley* returned to service.

In the 1950s and early 1960s the Craigendoran paddlers rarely visited Millport, and it was unusual to find any steamer lying across the inside knuckle of the pier. This view dates from 1960, the year *Waverley* was fitted with radar. By berthing on the knuckle, probably on an afternoon cruise allowing her passengers time ashore, *Waverley* left the inside berth free for the puffer *Saxon* (right) and the 'wee ferries' *Ashton* and *Leven*. Meanwhile, other steamers could arrive and leave unimpeded on the other side of the pier.

*Waverley* steams into Dunoon on a summer's afternoon in the late 1950s, with the Cloch Lighthouse soaking up the sun on the Ashton shore and holidaymakers relaxing at the water's edge. The 1950s were a decade of peace and plenty on the Clyde. After post-war rationing the people of Scotland's urban centres rediscovered the joys of a seaside holiday, swarming to the coast in numbers not seen since the 1930s. In 1957 more than 4.3 million passengers travelled on Clyde services, taking advantage of a fleet of 20 and a range of excursions that put all corners of the Firth within reach of resorts such as Dunoon. In the 1960s, thanks to rising living standards and cheaper access to foreign destinations, Clyde resorts began a period of decline, the effects of which were to be sorely felt by the steamer fleet.

Bathed in morning sun, *Waverley* moves astern out of Berth A at Craigendoran, leaving *Maid of Argyll* in Berth B and a trio of fuel wagons on the pier at Berths C and D. Until the advent of the 'Maids' in 1953, the Clyde's north bank fleet consisted exclusively of paddle steamers, the waters around Craigendoran being too shallow for propeller-driven ships. The four *Maids*, shallow-draughted, manoeuvrable and more economical than their steam-driven fleet-mates, were useful for basic services but had limited accommodation. *Waverley* was to outlive them all in active service. She also outlived her 'home' at Craigendoran which, unlike the railheads at Gourock, Wemyss Bay and Ardrossan, had no vehicle ferry connection to prolong its existence. At a public inquiry into the pier's closure in 1972, the Caledonian Steam Packet Company said passenger numbers there had fallen from 87,000 in 1967 to 33,500 in 1972, incurring a loss of £82,000 for that year. The balance of shipping services on the Clyde was shifting irrevocably towards the carriage of vehicles. Since 9th October 1976, when the pier buildings were gutted by fire, the former LNER railhead has been a ghost of the past, with only decayed wooden piles sticking out of the water to remind us of its former glory.

*Jeanie Deans* and *Waverley* sit at parallel berths at Craigendoran on a summer's day in 1960, boasting the radar scanners that were fitted to all Clyde excursion steamers in the spring of that year. At 240 feet *Waverley* was 11 feet shorter than *Jeanie Deans* but took the lion's share of cruise work, often completing a 12-hour day while the older steamer contented herself with the pedestrian duty of sailing round Bute every weekday afternoon. This led to anomalies in pay: *Waverley*'s officers, who were paid overtime only for Sundays, were working much longer hours for the same salary as those on *Jeanie*. Conversely the deck crew, engine-room ratings and catering staff enjoyed higher overtime payments on the 'cruise' roster than their colleagues on the 'half-day' ship. The solution from 1961 was to have the two Craigendoran paddlers alternating their weekly rosters. In the 1950s *Jeanie* was generally reckoned to have performed poorly, but with a new captain and engineer in 1962, she regained some of her old vigour, and the way she held off *Waverley*'s challenge in a race from Gourock to Craigendoran on August 13th that year has passed into legend.

After the withdrawal of *Jeanie Deans* in September 1964, *Waverley* faced a new stablemate across the pier at Craigendoran – *Caledonia,* the first south bank 'interloper' to take up residence on the north bank of the Clyde. This photograph shows the two paddlers in the livery adopted by the Caledonian Steam Packet Company between 1965 and 1969, featuring a 'monastral blue' hull and a red lion crest on the funnels. Built in 1934 for the CSP, *Caledonia* had spent the late 1950s and early 1960s as Ayr excursion steamer. With her large single funnel and concealed paddle-boxes, she had less iconic looks than *Waverley,* but war service and the mantle of age had given her a lot of character. She proved a worthy successor to *Jeanie* until she too was withdrawn at the end of the 1969 season.

*Waverley* and *King George V*, both with caps on their funnels, sit alongside each other at Greenock during the winter of 1965-66. The veteran MacBrayne turbine steamer, based at Oban in summer, usually wintered in the East India Harbour, a few hundred yards east of the Albert Harbour, where this photograph was taken. Since the late 19th century the Albert Harbour had been a winter haven for Clyde excursion steamers. During those long, dark months many enthusiasts would make a pilgrimage to Greenock, where they could admire the steamers in silence and anticipate the summer days when their favourites would once again bustle with life. The harbour was closed in 1968 and filled in with rubble from the recently demolished Princes Pier buildings nearby.

In 1958 *Waverley* fell heir to a day trip from the coastal resorts to the heart of Glasgow. Begun the previous year by *Jupiter* and *Marchioness of Graham*, the Up-River Cruise was an immediate success. Excursionists had two and a half hours to explore the city, with the option of returning by train via Gourock, Wemyss Bay or Largs. As soon as everyone had disembarked at Bridge Wharf shortly before 2pm, the steamer would 'cant' in preparation for the return journey – a process under way in this photograph from 8th July 1966. It involved letting the bow swing out into the river until the point was reached where a rope from the other side of the steamer could draw her back to the quayside, facing downriver. The Up-River Cruise gave holidaymakers a wonderful opportunity to see the Clyde shipyards and docks, which still dominated the riverbanks: Cunard's *Queen Elizabeth 2*, for example, was at that time under construction at Clydebank. The building of the Kingston Bridge in 1969-70 put an end to the Up-River Cruise – as it did to all sailings from Bridge Wharf, which lies (in much-transformed state) about a mile upriver from *Waverley*'s current Glasgow base at the Science Centre.

In 1971 there was mounting speculation that *Waverley*'s days were numbered. Two years earlier the Caledonian Steam Packet Company and David MacBrayne Ltd had been incorporated, with the Scottish Bus Group, in a new Edinburgh-based state conglomerate, the Scottish Transport Group (STG), which embarked on a strategy of developing vehicle-carrying ferry services and axing loss-making excursion steamers. After the withdrawal of *Caledonia* in 1969 and *Duchess of Hamilton* in 1970 (when CSP hulls reverted to black), the Clyde was left in 1971 with just two steam-powered vessels, *Waverley* and *Queen Mary II*, both of which – as had long been the custom with the Clyde's excursion fleet – spent more months of the year laid up in harbour than at sea earning money. For the first time in her career *Waverley* lay overnight at Gourock, not at Craigendoran, and on July 15th she was blown against Arrochar Pier, damaging her foremast and part of her railings. After emergency repairs, she sailed for the rest of the season with a stump mast, giving her an uncared-for look.

This view of *Waverley*'s dining saloon in July 1971 is a reminder of how elegant the onboard restaurant experience was in the good old days. Curtains, coat-hangers, mirrors, flowers, tablecloths, silver cutlery, white-coated waiters, even a bell – all this bespoke an era before the advent of packaged sandwiches, frozen peas, plastic cups and single-portion wine bottles. There were at least four sittings each of lunch and high tea, served between 12 noon and 5.30pm, for which bookings had to be made at the purser's office. Tea, coffee, fizzy drinks ("minerals"), scones and biscuits were available in the ship's cafeteria, situated forward on the main deck where the Jeanie Deans Lounge is now situated. The sale of alcohol was confined to the bar on the lower deck aft.

To celebrate her 25th anniversary, a group of enthusiasts chartered *Waverley* on Sunday 22nd May 1972 for a cruise to Ormidale in Loch Riddon, where passengers were ferried ashore by *The Second Snark* (foreground). The pier, situated at a remote spot about two miles from the Kyles of Bute, had not received steamer calls since 1939. Built in the mid-19th century to service local estates, it was included in the Kyles of Bute run from Greenock's Princes Pier, and later Wemyss Bay, but in the 1930s demand petered out. In 2012 *Waverley* made a return visit to Ormidale, again with *The Second Snark* in attendance, as part of the Clyde River Steamer Club's 80th anniversary celebrations.

*Waverley* steams in to Rothesay Bay on 25th August 1972, resplendent with new foremast and paddle-boxes painted black with white and gold edging – the first fruit of a public campaign to save her from the breakers. The possibility that Britain's once-plentiful fleet of paddle steamers might soon be extinct had been slow to dawn on ship enthusiasts, but the formation in 1959 of the London-based Paddle Steamer Preservation Society had helped to raise awareness south of the border. In 1971 two young dynamos, Douglas McGowan and Terry Sylvester, formed the Waverley Study Group as a pressure group, and it was thanks to them that *Waverley*'s owners were persuaded to paint the paddle-boxes black, emphasising her 'unique' mode of propulsion. *Waverley* had only three days out of service in the summer of 1972, and ended it with three enthusiasts' charters. The campaign to make her a special cause was gathering momentum.

By 1973, when this photograph of *Waverley* at Lamont's Port Glasgow shipyard was taken, a dialogue – even a degree of trust – was developing between McGowan and Sylvester on the one hand, and the paddler's Gourock-based managers on the other. Rather than representing a thorn in the STG's side, the two commercially-minded enthusiasts had revealed the ship's potential as a heritage project, and the way she was marketed – as 'the last sea-going paddle steamer in Europe' – began to reflect that. In January 1973 the STG's Clyde and West Highland shipping interests were transferred to a new organisation, Caledonian MacBrayne Ltd, which adopted funnel colours of red and black top, with yellow discs encircling red lions. McGowan and Sylvester wanted *Waverley* to stand out from the rest of the fleet, and campaigned for her funnels to be painted red and black with white band – as in 1947, her first season. The experiment did not turn out as planned. During her overhaul at Lamont's in March and early April 1973 (next to *Loch Carron* on the slip), the funnels appeared briefly with a yellow band that looked quite alien. By the time she took up service on Easter Monday, her colours were the same as the rest of the fleet.

Pictured at Largs in the summer of 1973, with a large crowd on board and plenty more on the pier, *Waverley* looks in the peak of health: by general consent she was well suited to CalMac's colours. Her 1973 season was nevertheless a troublesome one, with a record number of breakdowns, mainly due to boiler trouble. This was the first year *Waverley* did not sail to Arrochar. As well as the traditional Round the Lochs cruise, her roster included a Friday cruise to Tarbert and a Sunday cruise round Bute, calling at Millport but not Tighnabruaich. Her final day under the CalMac flag was Sunday 30th September – round Bute with 470 passengers – after which she moved from Gourock to James Watt Dock, Greenock, to await her fate.

*Waverley*, on a cruise round Bute, steams past *Queen Mary II* in the west Kyle on 11th July 1973. For anyone vaguely aware of the steamer scene that summer, *Waverley* was more or less doomed – despite attempts by her popular master, Captain Hugh Campbell (right), to show her at her best. Official figures for the previous year revealed that Clyde excursion sailings had suffered a 20 per cent drop in passengers compared to 1971, while carryings on car ferry crossings continued to rise. Caledonian MacBrayne could not afford to haemorrhage money on a declining cruise market when investment was needed in vehicle ferry services. When Douglas McGowan was invited to CalMac's Gourock office on 22nd November 1973, he thought it was for another of the 'fireside chats' he and Terry Sylvester had been having with John Whittle, CalMac's general manager. Instead, they were handed the chance to buy *Waverley* for £1. The offer came as a complete surprise – and a shock. They had no experience of running ships and next to no money.

By 1973 the fleets of paddle steamers that had once adorned the estuaries of Britain had all but disappeared, and precedents for their preservation were few. *Waverley*'s former LNER stablemate *Jeanie Deans*, pictured under tow on the Thames on 10th June 1967, served as a warning. Sold off the Clyde in 1965 to a London businessman who renamed her *Queen of the South*, she was restored to her original colours and given a bow rudder to help navigate against the tide and river stream. Publicity brochures advertised "an atmosphere of leisurely luxury and charm reminiscent of traditional riverboat cruising" as she made her way from the Pool of London to Kent and Essex resorts. The reality proved less inviting. The ageing paddler suffered frequent breakdowns and cancellations, and was sold to ship-breakers in Belgium after only two summers on the Thames.

As a combined mechanism, the wooden floats and steelwork of *Waverley*'s paddles make for a method of propulsion at once simple and complex. The simplicity lies in the circular action of two paddle-wheels that push the water in one direction, thereby propelling the vessel in the other. The complexity lies in ensuring not only that the constituent parts work in harmony, but also that the 'drive' of each float is maximised. For this purpose a feathering mechanism was developed in the mid-19th century to enable the paddles to enter the water at the most efficient angle, with the tilt of each float controlled by a rod. One of the reasons for the failure of *Jeanie Deans*' Thames sojourn was her new owners' focus on cosmetics, instead of attending to the boilers and paddles, the malfunctioning of which led to her downfall. When *Waverley*'s new owners took her in hand in 1974, they were determined not to make the same mistakes.

*Waverley* lies astern of *Clansman* in Greenock's James Watt Dock on 26th March 1975, in the later stages of a transformation that would allow her, six weeks later, to make her first sailing under the flag of Waverley Steam Navigation Company (WSN), a company set up by the Paddle Steamer Preservation Society. The formal handover of the ship from CalMac to the PSPS took place at a ceremony at Gourock on 8th August 1974, during which Douglas McGowan handed a symbolic £1 to the chairman of the Scottish Transport Group, Sir Patrick Thomas (who had given McGowan the pound note beforehand). The STG's gift had an air of philanthropy, but it was taking no chances. Should the enthusiasts achieve the impossible and get *Waverley* back in service, they were forbidden by the terms of sale to operate in competition with CalMac or sell the vessel to a third party. In the nine months between the handover and her return to service, *Waverley* was surveyed and thoroughly overhauled, a process that included the removal of 20 sackfuls of soot from her boiler. Against a backdrop of tireless fund-raising, a clever publicity drive and a surprising amount of goodwill from companies and individuals, the ship could once again raise steam. On 10th May 1975, gleaming with a fresh coat of paint, *Waverley* was ready to begin the next phase of her life.

Of all *Waverley*'s captains, none did more to establish her as a commercial venture than David Neill (left). Pictured with Jimmy Addison, the ship's relief skipper in the early years of preservation, Captain Neill served as master from 1975 to 1997. As a young MacBrayne officer in 1969 he had got to know Douglas McGowan, and the two teamed up for what was to be an abortive attempt to buy the recently withdrawn paddle steamer *Caledonia*. That experience proved a useful 'dry run' for taking on *Waverley*. Despite the notorious 1977 Gantocks incident, when Captain Neill tried a short-cut off Dunoon and landed on the rocks, he had the skill and determination to make the most of *Waverley* and shake off the setbacks. Other masters associated with her in the past 25 years include Graeme Gellatly and Steve Michel (below left), the latter nicknamed 'Captain Cool', and Andy O'Brian and Luke Davies (below). Captain O'Brian, senior master since 2008, deserves credit for maintaining the ship's appeal in a leisure market that has radically changed since the early days of preservation. He faces greater scrutiny than his predecessors: the regulatory environment has tightened, and *Waverley*'s critics are not shy of voicing their opinions on social media.

*Waverley*'s engines, open for all to see, count as one of the most spectacular survivors of the steam age. Steam from the boiler (concealed in the compartment at the far right) passes along the white overhead pipe and down to the base of the engine, where it powers three magnificent pistons, positioned diagonally – a mid-19th century arrangement designed to keep the main engine-casting low, bolstering the ship's stability. Each piston is linked to a single shaft running the breadth of the ship, which turns the paddle wheels on either side. *Waverley*'s engines consume around 650 litres of fuel per hour of steaming – double the amount a diesel ferry of equivalent size would use, running at a slightly slower speed. The tradition of making a showpiece of paddle steamers' engines began in the 1880s, thanks to James Williamson, captain of *Ivanhoe* and later manager of the Caledonian Steam Packet Company. He transformed the boxed-in machinery of the older vessels into a smartly turned-out space where everyone could admire the powerful engine cranks at work. In the golden years of the Clyde steamers, 'seeing the engines' had more than one meaning: it became a euphemism for men visiting the bar, while women and children were left to entertain themselves on deck.

The upper reaches of the River Clyde sometimes freeze over in winter, as on this occasion early in 1978. *Waverley*, berthed at Anderston Quay next to Western Ferries' *Sound of Islay*, is being prepared for her first voyage round Land's End en route to the south coast. For weather protection steel shutters were manufactured to cover her main deck windows, and the sponson windows were replaced with portholes recovered from the Clyde Port Authority vessel *Torch*, which was being broken up at Dalmuir. Water-tight doors were also fitted to the openings onto the sponsons at both ends of the alleyways: these had the added benefit of keeping the interior warm. All this work paid dividends. On her inaugural south coast season *Waverley* carried 54,000 passengers in the space of three weeks, and the water-tight doors later proved useful during heavy weather on the Clyde.

*Waverley* lies at Weymouth in May 1979, with *Caledonian Princess* arriving from the Channel Islands. For her first 30 years *Waverley* never ventured beyond the Firth of Clyde. But in a sign of her new owners' growing confidence, she left Scotland for the first time in April 1977, the idea being to widen revenue-earning possibilities beyond the core 12-week Clyde season. Her short visit to Liverpool, Llandudno and Fleetwood did not earn much money but was a public relations triumph. In April and May 1978 she gave the first of what was to become a regular season of excursions on the south coast of England and on the Thames. Her inaugural Bristol Channel sailings were undertaken in 1979. In 1980 and 1990 *Waverley* visited the French coast to mark the 40th and 50th anniversaries of the Dunkirk evacuation, and in 1981, 1982 and 1984 she circumnavigated Britain, visiting the Humber, Tees, Tyne, Forth and Tay, and winning many new friends along the way.

With the exception of sailing through the Kyles of Bute, there are few *Waverley* experiences to match the thrill of passing beneath Tower Bridge on the Thames. In this photograph, taken on 3rd May 1980, *Waverley* is being turned by a tug in the Pool of London, prior to steaming past *HMS Belfast* and under the bridge: the two bascules are being raised in preparation. Despite heavy costs, *Waverley*'s Thames seasons have always been well patronised – not least because, thanks to canny timetabling, they give people in Essex and Kent resorts an opportunity to sail to the heart of London and back in a day. Latterly *Waverley*'s Thames and south coast visits have taken place in September and early October, prior to a final weekend of sailings on the Clyde. On her return north in 2012 she made her longest ever unbroken journey, leaving Southampton at 8.45am on October 19th and arriving back at Glasgow at 4.40am two days later.

Of all the pier-calls made by *Waverley* in her 40 years as a 'preserved' steamer, few have been more exotic than Otter Ferry on Loch Fyne, where she is pictured on 11th April 1993. The quay, situated a mile north of the village, near Largiemore, opened in 1900 – the Inveraray steamer *Lord of the Isles* used it for three years, and the Ardrishaig mail steamers *Columba* and *Iona* made occasional calls – but from 1914 until 1948 it was served only by cargo boats. *Waverley*'s call was the first for 45 years. Amazingly the privately-owned structure was still usable, thanks partly to the durability of the wooden support piles, made of greenheart, but also to preparatory work carried out by Captain Steve Michel. He travelled overland to inspect the decking, ordered 10 sheets of 8x4ft planking from a DIY store and made sure he was present, with *Waverley* fireman Willie Ross, when it was delivered. *Waverley*'s one-off visit was a huge success.

In two phases between December 1999 and June 2003 *Waverley* underwent a £7m rebuild at Great Yarmouth, involving the replacement of her funnels, paddle-boxes, deck-houses and much of her steel plating. The aim, achieved with remarkable success, was to restore her appearance as closely as possible to her original 1947 condition, to improve passenger amenities and allow her to comply with modern regulations. The man responsible for planning and supervising the rebuild was Ian McMillan (right), a marine and mechanical engineer from South Wales. After starting to work for Waverley Excursions Ltd in the early 1980s, McMillan (1954-2014) became operations director and then chairman. He immersed himself in every aspect of running the ship, tackling head-on the increasingly complex health and safety demands, as well as constant human resources problems and the challenges imposed by new alcohol licensing laws. Besides his technical skills, McMillan's leadership qualities proved crucial in driving through the changes necessary to extend the ship's working life.

Whenever Cunard's premier cruise liners visit the Clyde, *Waverley* makes a point of giving them a welcome. Along with visits by the Tall Ships, these events are red-letter days in her calendar, always attended by a capacity crowd. In the view above, off Greenock on 25th July 1990, the Clydebank-built *Queen Elizabeth 2* is framed by *Waverley* and CalMac's *Saturn*. Waverley Steam Navigation Ltd's relations with CalMac have blown hot and cold over the years, and the paddler is sometimes obliged to tailor her programme to the requirements of the ferry operator. Lochranza, a village tucked into the north-west corner of Arran, is one of her calling-points where pier improvements have been of mutual benefit (opposite). The wooden steamer pier closed in 1972, and it was only after a new concrete structure was built in 2003, primarily as an overnight berth for CalMac's Claonaig car ferry *Loch Tarbert*, that *Waverley* was able to resume calls. They are pictured together on 24th August 2003.

Caledonian MacBrayne

*Waverley*'s Saturday sailing down the River Clyde to the Kyles of Bute and back has traditionally been her busiest, no more so than on Bute Games day, when she can be guaranteed a full load. In this view of Rothesay Pier on 19th August 2006, she has just arrived from Glasgow. CalMac's *Ali Cat* lies astern in the middle berth and the car ferry *Bute*, new the previous year, is setting off for Wemyss Bay, while *Waverley* will shortly leave for Tighnabruaich. The scene is reminiscent of Rothesay's heyday in the late 19th and early 20th centuries, when crowds of Glaswegians headed for the Bute capital and steamers were constantly arriving at and leaving the pier. Since 2007, when an end-loading linkspan was installed at the east berth of Rothesay Pier, *Waverley* has berthed at the west end. Thanks to the support of Argyll and Bute Council, which owns Rothesay Pier, *Waverley* pays no berthing fees there.

As *Waverley*'s purser for 23 seasons, Jim McFadzean became a legend in his own lifetime. Pictured on a rare occasion when he wore full uniform (left) and entertaining passengers during the end-of-season cruise in October 2009 (right), he was one of the ship's greatest assets, using his commercial acumen to maximise income and maintaining a list of bus companies 'a mile long' in case back-up was needed for altered or cancelled sailings. A native of Ayrshire, Jim spent his early career in agriculture before applying for the purser vacancy on *Waverley*. Joining the ship on 29th April 1988 at Oban, he was handed the keys after a day's training and never looked back. Unlike the halcyon days of the Clyde steamers, when pursers mostly stayed inside the ticket-office, Jim never settled for being ship's banker. He radiated bonhomie at the gangway, acted quickly when things went wrong and generally made it his task to see everyone went home satisfied. His retirement in October 2010 was marked by a series of presentations and accolades celebrating his contribution.

One of the pleasures of a trip on *Waverley* is the chance to watch a ship being berthed the old-fashioned way. These two views at Brodick show Captain Steve Colledge on the bridge as the heaving line is thrown ashore (above) and a deckhand awaiting orders to tighten the rope on the steam winch (opposite). Handling a paddle steamer is an art form: they have a tendency to 'slide' when the engines go into reverse on the approach to a pier. In former times, when coastal excursion steamers were plentiful, budding officers had ample opportunity to learn how to manoeuvre the natural way – without propellers or bow-thrusters. With *Waverley* now the sole survivor, it has become increasingly hard to find personnel confident enough to take on the challenge and accept her old-fashioned quirks.

Passengers disembark from *Waverley* at the ferry pier on the Hebridean island of Coll. The steamer made her inaugural trip round the Mull of Kintyre in 1981, but it was not until 12th May 2002 that she first visited Coll, an island with a population of barely 200. Since then she has also become a welcome visitor to neighbouring Tiree, in each case giving a short non-landing excursion for islanders before returning to Oban. Clyde-based paddle steamers began trading to the West Highlands in 1818 and by the late 1820s there were regular services from Glasgow to Tobermory, Staffa, Skye and Stornoway, as well as from West Loch Tarbert to Islay. In 1830 *Foyle* – an open-decked steamboat less than half *Waverley*'s length – undertook ambitious all-in trips from Glasgow via Londonderry to Staffa and Iona. In the same year *Ben Nevis* was advertised to visit St Kilda. Facilities on board these ships were rudimentary. Our early 19th century forebears must have been hardy souls.

On 23rd April 2011 *Waverley* made her first, and so far only, visit to Rum during her annual Western Isles season. From Oban she steamed up the Sound of Mull and round Ardnamurchan Point, the westernmost tip of the British mainland, before heading north for the Small Isles, of which Rum is the biggest and most mountainous. With the ship at anchor in Loch Scresort, passengers were taken ashore by the Iona-based *Ullin of Staffa* – a manoeuvre that recalled the open-decked flit-boats used for landing passengers and cargo at small Hebridean communities in the 19th and 20th centuries. Rum was one of the last to be served in this way. The slipway there was built in 2003, enabling CalMac's Small Isles ferry *Lochnevis* to tie up alongside the breakwater and lower her stern ramp.

CalMac's Small Isles ferry *Lochnevis* sits at her overnight berth at Mallaig while *Waverley* puts a line ashore. The date is 8th May 2007 and the paddler has just returned from a cruise to Inverie, an isolated community on the north side of Loch Nevis (top right). From this angle the approach to Mallaig looks straightforward – but with prevailing winds from the south and west, and a rocky shore to the east, *Waverley* needs to make a confident landing on the end of the pier, then warp her bow round to the berth facing the camera. On departure, she will go astern to the left, before turning and heading south for Oban. Going astern in windy conditions is *Waverley*'s Achilles Heel: with a spade-like rudder at the stern and no bow rudder, she tends to 'hunt into the wind', swinging her stern round uncontrollably. Captain Steve Michel has described the difficulties this creates: "Once she starts going into a swing, she's hard to stop, so it's about keeping as much control as possible for as long as possible. If the ship starts going the wrong way, you have to stop her quickly and start making headway to regain directional control."

*Waverley* represents different things to different people. To the older generation she is a nostalgic throwback to childhood holidays, before the age of steam gave way to the soulless automation of the modern world. To the younger generation she is a colourful curiosity – a quaint, quirky, clanky mechanical miracle powered by paddles. For her critics – and they do exist – she is an anachronism, an outdated relic. But for anyone who steps aboard, *Waverley* offers a ticket to the wonders of our maritime heritage and coastal landscape. Without her, what opportunity would we have to sail down the River Clyde, through the Kyles of Bute or between the Cumbraes (pictured), soaking up some of Britain's most spectacular scenery from the vantage point of the sea? Viewed unsentimentally 'the world's last sea-going paddle steamer' is a steel box with timber decks and a cranky engine. But for many of those who come aboard, she has a living personality and a character all of her own. As long as *Waverley* brings enjoyment to people, she will be special.

Of all *Waverley*'s calling points in the 'preservation era', Millport's Old Pier long stood out as one of the most picturesque – but in her first 20 years she was seldom seen there. A closer association with the island town did not begin until 1967, after the withdrawal of *Talisman* as Cumbrae steamer, when *Waverley* inherited the popular Sunday afternoon cruise to Largs, Rothesay and the Kyles of Bute. In 1973 she made weekly calls on her cruise round Bute, but it was only in 1975, her first year in private hands, that *Waverley* became a fixture on the Millport scene – a wonderful sight as she swept into her berth at the heart of the town on a summer's day, bringing visitors from far and near. Millport responded with pier-side displays of Scottish country dancing and a welcome from the town's pipe band – always greeted with spontaneous applause onboard. In June 2014, barely 20 years after the Old Pier had been renovated at a cost of £600,000, North Ayrshire Council closed it, ending a tradition of steamer calls going back to 1833, when Millport's original pier was built.